HOW TO HIRE/ KILL A LAWYER

A Simple Guide

Michelle Berthiaume

Fyrecurl Publishing Group

The characters and events portrayed in this book are real but some of the names are changed as a matter of courtesy and privacy.

ISBN-978-1-7341197-2-5
ASIN-

Cover design by: Emily McNamee
Library of Congress Control Number:
Printed in the United States of America

CONTENTS

HOW TO HIRE/KILL A LAWYER

--- A Simple Guide

BY

Michelle Berthiaume, J.D.

ISBN 978-1-7341197-2-5

ASIN:

Fyrecurl Publishing Group
Attention: Managing Editor
3201 Bonham Ave.,
Temple, Texas 76502

This book is dedicated to: Addicus Finch[1]

Whose effect on a twelve-year-old boy growing up in rural America in the 1960's created an indelible obligation to stand up for the rights of others less fortunate, regardless of the cost.

Michelle Berthiaume, *Esq.* (2016)

QUOTES:

About Lawyers

The minute you read something that you can't understand, you can almost be sure that it was drawn up by a lawyer. ---Will Rogers

"Am I not destroying my enemies when I make friends of them?" ~ Abraham Lincoln

"The First thing we do. Let's kill all the lawyers." --William Shakesphere, Henry VI, Part II, Act IV

INTRODUCTION

So, you need help.

You went out after work to the Cock-L-Doodle-Doo with a few friends and had a few drinks—No—you had a beer or a single glass of house chardonnay and got pulled over by uniformed law enforcement twenty feet from your driveway. The Deputy Sheriff is a young, nervous man, new at his job. He went to school with your younger brother, Bruce, who used to viciously tease him about his bright red cheeks from a bad case of acne he suffered throughout high school, and Rosey won't give you a break when you 'stumble' during the sobriety test. You explain that you usually don't drink, you were wearing heels, only had one beer, and your grandfather, who raised you, died yesterday and you were out commiserating with friends. Rosey won't be moved—and insists you call him Deputy Rodney Pike. While hurriedly getting you in the back seat of his cruiser, he accidentally bumps your head and you develop a ringing in your ears that even after the headache settles down days later, it won't go away. It prevents you from sleeping well, and you spout off a tirade of unkind slurs at your spouse who now wants that divorce he or she's been putting off for the last three years waiting for a good excuse. You never needed a lawyer before. You don't know anyone who works in law. What will you do, call your mother?!!

You could hire that lawyer your co-workers insisted did a fairly good job negotiating their union contract? Your best friend, Stinger, suggests you get the same lawyer to do a bunch of cases you seemed to have been suddenly blessed with—to get a fantastic discount. Still confused? Well, congratulations, Hilda or Homer! You're not alone. Every day countless folk just like you are hit with the same 'bad' karma. Don't compound your problem by listening to your coworkers or Stinger and selecting the wrong lawyer.

This is your lucky day. Picking up this book was your first good break. Your Karma is not all bad. Buying this book is the smart decision that saves you countless dollars and many sleepless nights. Here, I will impart my many years of experience as a trial attorney in both civil and criminal law, and succinctly in plain language a fifth grader could understand, tell you *how to hire a lawyer* in the 5 most common situations that average folk may encounter in their busy lives at least once; criminal law, family law, probate, personal injury, and transactional. Further, as a *former* attorney, my only allegiance is to you, the reader.

In other words, unlike many attorneys who write self-help books, I am not selling anything. I am not trying to get you to hire me or refer you to any other person or firm. I am not giving you *legal advice.* Just pointing you in the direction to find someone who can best help you in that regard. And in the process may share a few insights using anecdotes from my own experience.

Good reading! And best of luck in your search!

PART I: INITIAL ANALYSIS -

CHAPTER ONE -

Do you need an attorney?

Most people know how to manage their day-to-day life. One such ministerial task is to buy groceries. You go to the pantry, cupboard, refrigerator, or bread box, and look inside. You observe what's there and more importantly, what's not. Ah, you notice there is no sourdough bread, almond milk, goat's cheese, smoked turkey sausage -- or bologna. (Not everybody eats healthy all the time). That was easy. Before you went shopping you determined your needs by observing, then you decided whether to buy the same edibles or not and perhaps where to shop. Your favorite Walmart? Do you hit the Farmer's Market on the weekend? Or perhaps, that new gorgeous Wegman's that just opened downtown? Simple, right? So why can't retaining a lawyer be that simple?

Well, it can be, but admittedly, hiring a lawyer is not something most people do every day unless you're a managing partner in a law firm, so you need a guide to educate yourself. Or you could ask Stinger, a coworker, or do some research online, all of which don't give you the warm-and-fuzzies your freedom, driving privileges, money and pursuit-of-happiness depend on.

Arguably, you're a smart gal, or guy. You bought this book for a reason. Famed educator, Andrew Carnegie paraphrasing Samuel Johnson, once said: "Knowledge is of two kinds, One, you either know it, or two, you know where to find it."[2] Having a guide gives you the tools to determine a better course of action, so at the end of the process you can feel assured you have made the right decision along the way. No regrets!

When your car breaks down, that's out of the ordinary. It's not your usual routine. It's unfamiliar to most of us, but it's not rocket science. Once you determined you're not that DIY guy, you look elsewhere for help. You can trust a referral from a reliable source, Mom, Dad, sister Kate, or big brother Bill, or look online for a top mechanic, or stop by the dealership.

As you recall, in our scenario in the introduction, you got arrested for DUI. In most jurisdictions, it's a substantial fine, coupled with some incarceration or probation, points on your license and future civil and criminal consequences. DUI statutes provide for increased fines, incarceration, and other conditions for repeat offenders. An adjudication to the charge affects your goals and employment and creates pecuniary, personal and social dilemmas. Will you need security clearances for employment? Or a special license, or safety devices installed on your automobile to lawfully drive in the future? Will it cost more money to obtain insurance down the road?

You may need a lawyer if you have no idea what it fully entails to admit guilt, pay the fines and move on with your life. A conviction on your record has serious ramifications. They may even withhold adjudication. Do you know what that means? What it entails, and that some jurisdictions do not recognize this designation? Will an adjudication of guilt, or not, affect your job opportunities later in life?

You may need one if you choose the alternative, trial. Unless you were that law school dropout that knew it all, you may not understand the rules of court. Criminal procedures can get complicated, particularly if you are not versed in the language of lawyers. And if that prosecuting attorney is as mean as she looks, you may feel intimidated. It would be nice to have someone in your corner.

Most average folk, even many above-average, will acknowledge they need some legal assistance to understand the consequence regarding all of their options. Even that law-school dropout. Everyone, no matter how educated or what their experience or employment, at one time or another, needs to get competent legal representation, especially when emotion can impair judgement.

You, or any lay person, may discern from the facts laid out in the introduction of this book that you may need a divorce attorney. How emotional is divorce? Fear, anger, and emotional trauma flare up from the ashes of a failed marriage, still floundering in the dying embers of a lingering love. An emotionally charged ember can burn everything in its wake. Could you face your significant other across the table on issues that matter? How to distribute the marital estate, settlement of debt, where the children will live and with whom and the amount of child support? Could you really be civil when everything you worked for is at stake? How do you hide your feelings from a discriminating magistrate or judge?

Perhaps you may have perceived that your injury, received upon being imprudently thrust into the back seat of a police cruiser by an angry deputy sheriff with a grudge against a family member, was not reasonable. The permanent ringing in your ears should be compensated for. Do you even know what kind of attorney specializes in suing government entities or officials? Do you recognize all the causes of action that arise from the particular facts of your case (see Introduction) to include tort actions, civil rights violations or statutory damages? If the answer is 'No' then it may be advisable to seek the assistance of counsel.

Whether you wish to represent yourself in any, or all the various legal matters that arise may depend on several factors. The first of which is affordability. Lawyers aren't cheap. That law school education was inexorably inflated by a system anticipating a share of that burgeoning profit garnered from those enormous settlements seen in the media albeit, by a select few. Regardless of how you proceed, don't let cheapness be your weakness. If you have disposable funds available, it may be advisable to use them to obtain help. You wouldn't operate on your daughter's appendix, or your wife's bunions, simply to keep your savings buoyant. How many times have you heard someone complain: I should have done this or that. If only I had known that or I coulda-shoulda-woulda done it differently. Really? If I knew then what I know now ... Excuse after excuse, ad nauseum.

All of that second guessing is for not, when you didn't have the money to hire one in the first place. Obviously, this book (How to Hire a Lawyer/a Simple Guide) is designed for someone who already decided to hire one and was smart enough to gain some insights before doing so. However, for the sake of avoiding those woeful questions of regret later, let's examine the other side of the coin.

In any case, you have the right to represent yourself, with some limitations in criminal matters that go beyond the scope of this book. This book merely provides information but does not advise, nor does it purport to make judgments for you. It's informative. A simple guide. Read it and extrapolate relevant information that may help you when you do decide to hire legal counsel.

CHAPTER TWO -

Self-Representation vs. Legal Counsel

In criminal matters, like the DUI introduced earlier, you will have to determine whether to represent yourself, or to hire an attorney. You can even elect to represent yourself in civil matters, although this right is vehemently discouraged by many courts when trials are a necessary consequence to an action.

Often, in criminal matters, the court will conduct a small hearing to determine whether you are competent to understand the consequences, and whether you are capable of following basic court etiquette and procedure. Many times, a counsel will be appointed to assist people who lack some of the requisite tools required to meet the court's minimum comfort level. Courts will often want to avoid errors that would cause the case to be overturned.

Ah, but you're intuitive, smart, and analytical. Not much is missed when you look at things closely. You love riddles and puzzles and often guess the ending to a good who-dun-it on the television. Why spend good money on an attorney when you are smart enough to analyze the situation yourself and get it over with.

Most people aren't that astute. They don't catch every nuance that may affect their current or future rights. Even attorneys, judges, or legislators (the guys that wrote and enacted the laws), may need help. Experienced legal professionals can forget to look carefully at all the facts of a case. They miss things. Sometimes, even in the minutest details hiding in the minor charges that might mess up their career down the road. It is not possible to be all knowing Particularly in subjects you are unfamiliar, nor have the education. It is also difficult to set aside emotion when so much is at stake. Still, some situations or consequences are almost impossible to imagine. The ability to correct errors in judgment that arise after something has happened might be helpful.

Generally, in the United States and a few other countries, at the behest of any criminal action, you will be assigned a public sector attorney as a precautionary measure to protect your rights. Your appointed representative will review your paperwork to see whether probable cause (a good reason) existed for your arrest. In-other-word's there must be some facts articulated in the arrest report revealing the officer observed a crime was committed and that *you* committed the crime. Such findings are necessary under our laws, to arrest and continue to hold someone criminally liable for the crime.

This initial determination is required by our Federal and State Constitutions. In fact, most of the Free World and some not so free, abide by the same or similar principles for holding you in detention or in the continued prosecution of a case. Law enforcement officers cannot go around arresting people simply because they had a grudge against you or some family member who had taunted them in high school. Some Jurisdictions call this First Appearance. Others use different terms. Assuming this threshold is met, there is a presumption of innocence that requires release, either with or without some form of security; a bond or promise on recognizance. Some incentive to ensure that you will return to court to face the charges.

Assuming the DUI was a first infraction, it would likely be a misdemeanor. A plea offer by the court may be the payment of minimal fees under the statute. The high costs and time spent obtaining an attorney may prompt some to just get it done.

Why throw good money after bad you may think. Innocent or not, it is a lost cause. The arresting officer, the Judge and even the prosecuting attorney would advise you of your right to seek legal counsel before you enter a plea to a criminal charge. The court will advise you of your rights to counsel again at sentencing and right to an appeal.

Should you stand before a court later at trial you will be reminded again of a right to counsel. If you persist in representing yourself, a small hearing would be had, ensuring you are legally competent to make that choice. Competence and informed consent are the mainstays of American jurisprudence.

CHAPTER THREE –

An Attorney's perspective (an anecdote)

In my first trial out of law school as public defender, I represented a cherubic, young man who, at 30, still lived at home with his disabled father, and mother. He was charged with a First and a Second-Degree Misdemeanor.

Michael Gnome was insecure and introverted. His dream was to become a police officer. He had obsessed over wearing a badge ever since he was a child. He was broad and stocky, and built like a linebacker, but more designed for a high school football team. Michael, for all his valiant efforts, lacked some of the more salient traits that would have helped him realize his dream. Michael failed the police exam three times. But he wasn't dissuaded. He intended to try again the next year.

In the meantime, Michael kept his hair buzz-cut short. He went to a gun range with his dad every Tuesday evening to decimate clay pigeons. He bought an unmarked police cruiser at the city auction; an old white, Ford Grand Marquis. He later mounted a CB radio/scanner that he bought at the local Radio Shack. Michael even donated money to the local branch of the Police Athletic League. He proudly displayed his PAL sticker with the badge insignia, stuck firmly on the back bumper of his car. Michael liked to go to car shows held in the parking lot of a local diner to show off his old cruiser. When he went, he always wore his favorite dark blue sweatshirt, brazenly embossed in large white letters on the back: "Bustin' Ours Savin' Yours."

One evening after the car show, Michael decided to run to the mall to buy a gift for his father's birthday. He got there late. Stores had closed for the evening. He sat behind the wheel of his used cruiser in the parking lot, dreamily looking out at the traffic on the busy street in front of the mall. He sat a bit too long, he admitted. He drew the attention of a passing mall security guard who drove his car up next to Michael's refurbished cruiser to chat.

When the security guard realized he had mistaken Michael for a real police officer, he ordered him out of his car and arrested him for impersonating a law enforcement officer. Afterwards he discovered the CB radio was tuned into a police channel, a second-degree misdemeanor punishable by a $500 fine and up to 60 days in county jail. Fortunately, Michael did not get charged with unlawful possession of two shotguns and buck shot ammunition he kept separately in the trunk. He had the proper permits. However, it added more punch to the case against him.

After a prolonged 12-hour trial, Michael was found Not Guilty of the first-degree charge of impersonating a law enforcement officer. Unfortunately, the jury found him guilty of the lesser charge: possession of a "police scanner." There wasn't much we could argue about saving Michael from the consequences of the second charge. He did *possess* a scanner (albeit bought lawfully at Radio Shack) and it was tuned into a police channel. The case seemed pretty cut and dry.

Even my supervisor, Bea Taquachel, who had been sitting Second-Chair with me, thought it was a lost cause. She told me not to waste time on the second charge but to concentrate on the more serious First-degree charge, where he could have been sentenced to one year in the County jail and ordered to pay a $1,000 fine. There was no defense--Or *was* there?

Nearly a year later I was in another county defending two black youths in Juvenile court for obstruction of a Law Enforcement Officer (LEO) in the line of duty. The teenaged brothers were sitting on the back of their friend's car on the side of the road waiting for their friend to come back from the beach, when a uniformed beach patrol guy came pedaling up the hill and ordered them to: "Get off the car!"

One brother complied, the other laughed and refused to move. He arrested both black youths. He claimed to have a legitimate fear that they were intimidating him by laughing. It interfered with the performance of his duty—writing tickets. It made him nervous, he said.

While waiting to argue my client's case before the judge, I busied myself looking at the statutes. It clearly stated: 'anyone opposing a certified law enforcement officer in the performance of his duty was guilty of a First-degree misdemeanor, obstruction of justice.' I noted the cool blue and white trimmed uniform the beach patrol guy was wearing. He looked like a police officer but was he, an employee of the city of Naples, a *Certified* officer as defined in the statute? To be certified, one had to attend an accredited police academy and be sworn in (take an oath to defend the constitution and all of the state laws. I waited until trial to trigger the Double Jeopardy clause. The state presented its case then; I asked him on cross examination:

"Sir, have you ever been to the police academy?"

"No, Ma'am."

"Have you taken an oath to defend the constitutions of

the United States or of the state of Florida?"

"No, Ma'am."

"Then, how can you be a certified law enforcement officer?"

"Ma'am?" He hadn't a clue what I was getting at.

Neither did the Judge or state attorney. No one had any idea what it meant.

I moved for a Judgement of Acquittal for lack of jurisdiction. The judge granted the motion after I read the statute in open court on the record. It turned out the beach patrol guy was not a certified law enforcement officer. No crime had been committed.

He was a city employee. More similar to a security guard employed by a mall than a policeman. Neither needed to be a *certified law enforcement officer.* Non-certified officials usually perform preparatory training or administrative functions, and they lack general arrest authority. The Beach patrol guy had been a salesman on his uncle's used car lot prior to taking the job for the City of Naples. His duties consisted mostly of ticketing illegally parked cars along neighborhood streets and roads leading to the beach. He was a snappily dressed meter-maid.

I called Michael Gnome the next day and we filed a motion on his behalf to expunge the record. He had already paid the fine and successfully completed his probation. The judge granted the motion. I could not ethically move to set aside judgment. As it turned out, the mall security guard who arrested Michael, was an off-duty deputy sheriff moonlighting to make extra money. He was certified law enforcement officer as defined in the statute. Michael and his parents were satisfied with the expungement of his record. It allowed him peace of mind, and a continued hope of realizing his dream of someday becoming a certified law enforcement officer.

This anecdote elucidates the need for assistance of counsel. Even experienced lawyers fail to perceive every detail of a case. There is a reason they call it the practice of law. Here educated and experienced professionals versed in aspects of the law that average, or even above-average people like you, may not be aware that substantially affects your rights. That being said, many still choose to represent themselves. Not a problem. It's your right. You are an adult. You can make that decision.

Like I told my granddaughter when she chose to drop out of George Mason University. Cassie had a full ride, all tuition and books and living quarters, paid by her aunt "the Colonel". She wanted to move in with her Bolivian boyfriend (who worked in a pet store). There are no right or wrong decisions in life, I sagely explained. Only some more obdurate than others.

"It's just a speed bump. Honey. You slow down, hit the bump, then proceed to get on with your life. You go in whichever direction you choose to drive and carry whatever load that decision gave you."

Obviously, some decisions are harder than others. Nearly a year later, my daughter, April, called to ask:

"When I dropped out of grad school and moved in with what became: 'that wonderful son-in-law,' and I asked you for a loan, you told me: 'You made your bed, now sleep in it.'"

"Why, sweetheart, you're the parent. I am Cassie's, Mimi. Your job is to raise her. Mine is to encourage and spoil her."

"Well, Mimi, your granddaughter needs some encouragement. I'll text you her new phone number." April's voice was tainted with a touch of mischief.

"Why, what happened?" I was worried.

"She got into a fight with her boyfriend and is moving back in with Jackie. She needs help to move her stuff. Jim and I are working. So, this sounds like your job—go spoil her."

"But I'm working and live in Texas, and she lives in D.C.!"

"Ha!" April laughed. "You made this bed..."

How was I to know when I told Cassie it was okay to drop out of a top college and move in with her Bolivian boyfriend, he lived with his parents, two male cousins, three dogs and a pet pig, in a modest two-bedroom house in the suburbs of D.C. She and her boyfriend, Marcello, occupied a bed in the middle of the kitchen. I took time off from work, drove 1,400 miles to help Cassie move back in with her Aunt Jackie, a colonel at the Pentagon, who refused to take the dog into her new home.

"What am I going to do with a dog?" I was exacerbated.

"But Mimi," Cassie pleaded, "She's a golden Doodle. Only a mid-size dog, and so sweet."

"I-I haven't had a dog in over twenty years." I stammered.

"I can't let her go back to the pet store. She may not get adopted. They'll put her down. I'll have to get my own apartment."

"Ok, I sighed.

We had a dog when the kids were small. Cassie's mother pleaded similarly to take in a stray. The pup showed up at our back door one winter. It was the cutest little thing with one blue eye and one brown, and so smart the kids named him: Einstein.

"See, he can sit up and beg." April had pleaded, standing behind her older sisters, Jen Rose and Jackie.

I looked down at a shaggy little brown and grey pup sitting on his haunch with one paw in the air. They're cute when they are small. He grew up to be a sixty-pound Coy-dog, half coyote and part husky. We didn't get fined by the game warden until he started bringing deer down on his own.

"Ah, Cassie---" I was flummoxed.

"Yes, Mimi."

"Why are you bringing the dog over to me at 4:00 a.m. Why can't I pick her up on the way out of town?"

"Because that's when Marcello is sleeping."

"Huh?!"

There are inevitably and invariably subtle facts that ooze to the surface of any case. Usually, unexpectedly and without any warning. The mid-size dog turned out to be a black flat-coated, Golden-Doodle. Bella was gnarly, flea-infested, and overweight. Mid-sized? She was almost 65 pounds. Not the smaller end of the breed that I had expected, and unlike her lighter relatives, she shed. Big, black, wooly-boogers flew off her back as soon as she jumped into the back seat of my car.

We've found in the analysis that several factors

would influence a reasonable person not to represent himself and to hire an attorney. Knowledge, emotion, and what my Japanese grandmother would have called (if I had one): Hitsuzen. So, an unforeseen or necessary Zen consequence of an action. One would have to be an experienced attorney to have anticipated it or a seer. For the sake of avoiding all of those indelicate questions that come from regret later, we ask, what is an attorney anyway? What makes them special?

CHAPTER FOUR -

Attorneys—A Brief History

Before 41 AD, in Ancient Greece, and later in Rome, persons were expected to come before or answer to some authority whenever a conflict arose between them and another citizen, a foreigner, or the governing authority: City-State, Emperor, or local prefect. Informal orators who understood laws could articulate the issues better than an average citizen. These "friends of the court" were allowed to stand up to speak on another's behalf.

Advocates evolved in Rome, without formal regulation, who not only spoke for someone but were knowledgeable in the law sufficient to present evidence, legal theories, cross-examine witnesses, and to argue before the magisterial body. Shortly after, regulations further defined the role of an orator and advocate and evolved into the legal profession we have today.

Centuries ago, much of the world population was uneducated. Common folk needed someone literate and who could write in order to conduct business. These scribes prepared documents and interpreted writings. Esquire evolved from the squire, a servant to a Knight and usually Nobility of landed gentry. The title demarked their status as under a gentry class but above a commoner or serf. As literacy grew, the terms for squires (landed gentry) merged with scribes (literate/knowledge) where both began to serve the commoner who needed legal assistance with (the Crown) or ecumenical (the Church), using their expertise and training.

Today, attorneys are called by various names throughout the world including barrister, solicitor, counselor, lawyer, advocate and esquire. Their role is still one to advise, and to speak (argue) on behalf of some public or private authority, business entity, or some individual, who needs legal assistance.

Judges, magistrates, prosecutors and public defenders are generally lawyers, people who have graduated from an accredited college or university. Not everyone who works in law graduated from law school. Arbitrators, mediators, and administrative judges are not necessarily lawyers. However, they usually have specialized training to allow them to make decisions on particularized legal matters.

CHAPTER FIVE -

The Evolution of Law.

In Great Britian and the United States, and many other countries around the world, common law drives a system of justice that keeps order in the community. It derives from the doctrine of stare decisis or a basis of legal decisions or customary rules rather than created statutes or regulations. It evolved during medieval times when the monarchy ceded its waning powers to legislative bodies that began running governments.

In England, the Magna Carta drained the monarchy of its ability to make or enforce laws, without the guidance of the people, namely the merchants who controlled the wealth of the county at the time. Further, the Churches powers to decide ecumenical transgressions passed down and eventually merged with the jurisdiction of magistrates and judges that oversaw civil infractions and crimes. Thus, many of our laws are influenced by religious tenets.

I am often asked by people who are not educated in the law, how it works, or how it evolved. They want me to define the principles that make order in a civilized society —the rule of law---and they are surprised to learn the theories derive from early religious tenets. All men are created equal. Good inevitably triumphs over evil. Law and justice should be synonymous. Peace will prevail and chaos, if not tamed, at least will be contained. Even righteousness is tempered by mercy. Something right out of the bible.

These tenets have been threaded into our legal system through the ages. They end up, not just expressed, but implied in the context of our laws, statutes, and regulations. The rules that run our daily lives appear to be written into our DNA. Such beliefs are ingrained into all humanity. Inscribed on our hearts by God.

For those agnostic readers who share no such belief, understand that your value-system's origins are influenced by our faithful forefathers who disciplined their children to follow these moral precepts. Inside each responsible person is a faith in the integrity and goodness of mankind. It's inherent in our core beliefs, even when we fail to believe in the existence of an eternal being. Think of it as honed over centuries of canonical rearing. A moral compass for comparison and weighing consequences of ours and others' actions---set towards true North—righteousness.

Presumably, you believe that everyone is born knowing the difference between right and wrong. That compassion, mercy and altruism oozes naturally from humanity like a weeping wellspring, that in some, is stopped up with fear, hurt, or anger created by an intemperate upbringing or life experience. Generally, our laws are not steeped in strict liability that righteousness would demand, an objective punishment like 'an eye for an eye,' so to speak. A few strict liability laws are enacted for policy considerations. Usually, where the loss of life could be catastrophic. Like carrying a gun onto a passenger aircraft. However, our common law influenced most legislation, so laws have evolved to take into consideration the flawed character of mankind.

Criminal statutes have a discretionary, more subjective process that considers the imprudent judgments humans often make, like drinking and driving. Crimes are often divided into degrees and classifications that consider the level of harm. Simple assault to Homicide. Misdemeanors versus felonies; levels of intent—from manslaughter to premeditated murder. Criminal liability based upon the values of property and levels separated by the value of the damages—petty theft versus grand theft, criminal mischief all the way to arson.

Another (mercy) mitigation in our laws is founded upon the age of defendants—juvenile versus adult crimes, and the competence of a defendant. Defenses for criminal liability that consider the sanity of an individual and levels of intellect, incapacitation--all the way to mental retardation—er—intellectual disability.

In our society, even punishment is relegated to provide for leniency. Biblically speaking, righteousness tempered by mercy (an undeserved grace). These may have stemmed from our common law proprietary, pecuniary and personal interests when mixed with an ecumenical confluence. Evidence of mitigation assists the magistrate or judge to determine the type, severity, and length of time of incarceration, or whether probation will suffice to satisfy the law based on the unique circumstances present in every case. All of which requires a person to possess sufficient understanding of his or her decision to self-represent or otherwise obtain the assistance of a counsel.

The concept of self-representation in our jurisprudence arises from this understanding that a competent person may opt to do so, after a brief review by an impartial magistrate or judge. In most criminal matters and certain civil matters, you will be able to represent yourself, once you have been appraised of the consequences. Albeit it is not possible to know all that may arise.

It is always advisable, in any situation where the

need arises to participate in a legal action, to obtain competent legal counsel. A person trained or at least exposed to the nuts and bolts of the law. Particularly where it affects one's livelihood, liberty, health, family, employment, money, reputation, and future.

The intricacies of law are so diverse and procedures that deliver them evolved with such complexity, that in conformity with the old adage: 'Only a fool represents himself' is applicable. It is also recommended that even the most astute lawyer not attempt to represent himself, lest he has 'a fool for a client,'

PART II –

STRUCTURES OF REPRESENTATION

CHAPTER SIX:

Types of Lawyers

We've answered a few questions and demonstrated why it is not wise to represent yourself in matters where (1) you are not knowledgeable, (2) where emotion can taint your judgment, and (3) where Hitsuzen (predestined; Japanese) or (4) Sabba (Yiddish) an unknown consequences can arise affecting your legal rights. This is true, regardless of whether you enter a plea or go to trial and even after judgement or a decision is made in a case. When you better understand the types of lawyers and what they do, you will be able to find the right attorney for your matters with confidence. Although they have similar training and pass the same bar exam, not all lawyers do the same thing.

If you've followed the reading up to this point, you have a better understanding of the various nomenclatures used to describe legal professionals world-wide. The terms to describe lawyers have also gone through changes. Scribes, Squires, and those later referred to as Esquire to show elevation of status. This happened as lawyers' duties merged and evolved over the centuries and customs devolved and became forgotten. The terms took on a new meaning. Esquire now is associated with a practicing member of the bar, authorized to represent clients in court. Lawyer (as a broader term) is used to describe someone who graduated from an accredited law school and is knowledgeable in the law. He or she is limited to research, writing, and other disciplines that do not require representation of clients in court, nor can they give legal advice to a client. When a lawyer passes the bar and is a member, she becomes an attorney and may use Esquire behind her name. Only a member of the bar is eligible to represent clients in court. Juris Doctor (J.D.), showing the educational level may be used by law graduates.

That isn't to say that a J.D. cannot operate in court as an attorney but must be certified by the court or by special rule approved by the bar or state of jurisdiction that allows this temporary role. They would still use the designation Juris Doctor (J.D.) to reveal their status. An attorney is the term used to describe a lawyer who is a member of the bar, certified to practice within a certain jurisdiction (state or federal court) and will have the designation Esquire (Esq.) behind their name denoting their status. Attorneys are lawyers authorized to represent clients in court and can give legal advice. It should be noted that Lawyer, at least in American jurisprudence has been so synonymously used with attorney that any distinction is obscured.

Now you know how they evolved, who they are, and what they do, or do you? Only about 60% of law school graduates go into traditional roles practicing law. Statistically, the American Bar Association estimates about 70% of attorneys are in private practice and of that number less than 20% have a general practice, where they practice across the broad spectrum of legal miasma. Most attorneys or firms will handle one or several types of law, but not every kind of thing where a legal conflict or transaction needs administration. Although attorneys are supposed to be able to make themselves reasonably competent to represent in any subject matter, reality dictates discretion.

As many categories of law, there are as many kinds of

lawyers who practice within them. Corporate lawyers may be attorneys or not and fall within the umbrella of corporate law. Some specialize in litigation, others in real estate, or other specialty law. Some are litigators, others transactional specialists, still others operate as paralegals or perform other ministerial duties. There are family lawyers, who are attorneys who represent clients in various family issues, some are mediators, and some magistrates working in a family court.

Probate attorneys handle the filing of documents in the administration of probate matters. While other lawyers become specialists in creating estate plans and trusts and if they are attorneys, they would advise clients accordingly and represent them in court. There are some attorneys who specialize just in litigation matters arising from probate or poorly drafted estate plans. Thus, there are various types of lawyers available to assist in your legal matter arising from the particular facts of your case. Such as the death of your grandfather—who raised you—but say never adopted you.

The question now becomes, which type of lawyer do you need. Let's say you have a modest income and savings and want to be frugal but not foolish. Which type of firm would produce the best attorney for the money?

CHAPTER SEVEN –

Large corporate and smaller boutique law firms

I had a friend once who, whenever she debated whether to spend money recalled the advice her father gave her: "Don't let cheapness be your weakness". You get what you pay for. You buy a cheap attorney; you get a cheap attorney. Most of us would opt to pay a little more for better representation. So where do we find the best attorney to handle your case or cases? And is cost really the best way to determine whether an attorney is good or not?

A Cadilac costs more than a Subaru. Both will get you where you want to go. However, if you really want to go in style--private firms pay more and generally lure more experienced and presumably smarter attorneys to work for them. Many come from the more reputable legal institutions, Harvard, Yale, or Penn State and the list goes on. But don't they all have to pass the bar? Doesn't that indicate a lawyer is ready to handle any case? Absent some specialty law areas, like patent law, yes. Once a lawyer graduates from an accredited university or college, he or she is expected to research the issues in a case to become reasonably competent to represent a client.

Admittedly, the quality of the education, as in any field of study, is worth consideration. However, would you hire a jet propulsion engineer to fix your lawn mower? Is it really necessary to hire Allen Dershowitz or Clarence Darrow, on your first DUI? Well, I suppose, if you were wealthy enough you could put together that dream team. Should we ask O.J. Simpson or Michael Jackson, for a referral? Or perhaps we could ask another notorious 'wealthy' client, like Von Bulow. Celebrations aside, you may spend more money than the case is worth, unless, like the noted gentlemen, it's a matter of life (in prison) or death.

Large firms employ numerous attorneys and legal professionals. All with varying degrees of expertise that better cover a wider spectrum of the legal goals of the firm. The newer lawyers and paralegals usually spend a lot of their time creating billable hours for the more lucrative cases and grind away at the lesser cases, to gain more experience. Big firms usually have larger expenses and are profit driven. Most cater to more affluent clients because they need more money to keep the doors open. The state bar has rules that govern a lawyer's obligation to perform community service hours, and some get appointed to conflict cases after the Office of regional counsel. But I wouldn't hold your breath.

In your first DUI matter introduced earlier, you would be lucky not to get one. Many attorneys working in a large firm have never had an appointed criminal case much less worked in criminal law. Usually, larger firms opt to pay a fee on behalf of their attorneys to the bar in lieu of the community service requirement. This means your chances of getting one of the more expensive attorneys on the cheap are minimal.

Even in civil matters, when a client comes into the office of a large firm, they are screened by a paralegal or a legal assistant then assigned one of the many attorneys in the firm. Would it surprise you to learn that your case is not necessarily assigned according to its complexity, but on the projection of time, expense and estimated profit. Also, the billable hours and the costs of retainers outprice the average person looking for an attorney. So, that settles it. Affordability plays a big part in the attorney you hire. The $5,000 to $7,500 retainer you may have to pay a large firm would swallow up the total costs of your entire matter's fines and court costs.

The smaller boutique firms that specialize in criminal law and possibly handle a few other areas of law may be a better bet for your case, or maybe not. There are fewer attorneys to choose from, but usually at lower costs. Additionally, you are more likely to meet your attorney in person prior to going to trial. There may be more intimacy in a smaller firm. Albeit, it has less resources at its disposal. There is something to be said about having direct access with the attorney who will be arguing your issues before a court.

Talking to the team of paralegals and lesser attorneys in a large firm may give you the feeling they got your issues well covered. If you think, the more the merrier you're sadly mistaken. It just means that the attorney handling your case is so busy with several other more pressing matters that he has his team working on yours and others until it's time for disposition.

Usually, in a first DUI, regardless of whether it is a strong case or not, it will end on a motion (based on some technical issue, like illegality of the arrest) or in a plea. Sometimes in a plea bargain to a lesser charge like reckless driving, if the firm has a good relationship with the prosecuting attorney.

Although the smaller firm or individual attorney that specializes in criminal law may give you more personal attention, he too, is likely to pursue a course of action that quickly disposes of his case load. Ah, but the cost is so much less than that dream team. That isn't to say that there aren't a few attorneys out there available to take your case in a direction that has your best interests at heart. Most do---or believe they do. We will examine how to find *that* attorney after further analysis.

Is a private attorney better than a publicly appointed one? That is a hard question to answer. Is a large law firm better than a small one? All are interested in moving their caseloads in the most efficient and productive way practicable. How do we find an attorney that considers your individual interests over the pecuniary considerations of our contemporary law practices? The answer is always relative. It depends on the quality of the people that practice within that organization.

Firms may advertise that they have 150 or more combined years of experience. Often, firms that boast large settlements in personal injury cases or about the combined number of years the total number of practicing attorneys in their firm is misleading. At best, it's mere puffery. If experience were the only indicator of quality representation, then there would be no new attorneys in private practice. Although all attorneys are required to take continuing education courses to keep themselves abreast of changes in the law, young attorneys are already familiarized after completing an updated curriculum. In many cases, it's nice to have someone whose confidence is earned by years of practice, but it falls short of defining whether he is the right attorney for you. Size of a firm, number of years of experience or results might be one indicator but it's not infallible.

CHAPTER EIGHT -

Publicly appointed vs. privately retained counsel

As a lowly public defender, I once filed and argued a motion that contained elaborate case law proving my point with a majority opinion and strong legal precedent that would certainly win on appeal. My opponent with several years of experience more than my six months argued: "Judge, that's just the way we've always done it. We've never needed a warrant, and we have been serving papers on defendants in this county for hundreds of years." He presented no case law, merely local custom, and familiarity. He won for the moment, but the appeal came back in my client's favor.

As young lawyer in the public defender's office, I won several appeals and set state case law, and I had more trials in my first year than any other attorney, private or otherwise, experienced or novice, that extended to five counties in Southwest Florida. My win loss records were impressive, but I did not win them all. Sometimes success is not always measured in wins over losses. An attorneys' sacred obligation extends to zealously represent clients to pursue their interests to ensure they achieve the full due process of law guaranteed by our constitution.

Many are satisfied they had someone that listened to them. Someone who believed in their case. Someone who kept them informed, responded timely to their concerns and consulted them on decisions to be made. An attorney they felt confident gave them her best efforts. In my years of experience, although I won more trial than I had lost, I could never tell someone that I could win their case. Never. All I could ever say to them is that I would do my best. So, where does the average Jane or Joe, like you go about finding the best lawyer for their case?

I think it is clear from the reading thus far that you need an attorney in some if not all of the areas highlighted in the introduction. The threshold question becomes: can you afford an attorney? If so, what kind of attorney do you need and second, where do I find one? Do I go to the private sector or stay with the free public appointed counsel, if eligible.

CHAPTER NINE -

Criminal Law

At First Appearance you filled out paperwork so the court could determine your financial situation, and whether it qualified you for public appointment of counsel, and for a minimal fee or not.

The Office of the Public Defender may have just the right attorney for your case, or maybe not. It generally pays its attorneys a competitive wage but often less than other private law firms. It hires its legal professionals from across the spectrum of accredited law schools and selects students that are ranked from best to least in their classes. Thus, like the other comparisons between large and small firms, it makes the quality of education at least a consideration. The Public Defender's Office has all of the financial resources of government that may match the larger firms in paying the expenses of a case, but subject to government regulation, oversight, and moderation.

One of the greatest assets of a public domain appointment of counsel is its experience level. Across the broad range of criminal, juvenile, guardianship and certain other civil matters, the Public Defender and Offices of Regional Counsel, handle more cases than any other private organization or attorney that practices in its jurisdiction. It becomes a problem, when the case load of impoverished people in need of an appointed attorney becomes so great it overwhelms the offices' budgeted resources.

Attorney caseloads can be nearly unmanageable.

They often resort to a system many attorneys have coined: "human trafficking". They usually plea out all but the hard-core cases that carry severe penalties and jail time. You're meager first-time DUI becomes a case management problem for their office. There will be pressure to dispose of your case as soon as possible. But you're innocent, you explain. It's not fair! Well, take heart. Attorneys may be employees of the firm or office, but they're professionals, that follow a code of ethics. The prosecutor has a legal and ethical duty to use his or her prosecutorial discretion that would not offend the constitutional parameters and the oath of office each one takes upon appointment.

Similarly, the public defender, or appointed counsel, must ethically handle your case or be subject to professional and legal ramifications. Some may affect their ability to practice law. In some cases, bad judgement in handling matters for clients in and out of court may subject them to criminal prosecution. There were several young attorneys and some more experienced ones I had known in Florida who faced charges in federal court after mishandling financial and real estate matters that had questionable origins and designs. Each individual attorney has his or her own moral code, that one would hope exceeds the minimal prescriptions of their Bar's code of ethics.

In the matter of Michael Gnome's[3] case as outlined earlier, it was unheard of in the courthouse that a misdemeanor trial would go much after six and certainly not twelve hours. There were many side bars suggesting I 'move it along' by the judge. However, my idea of justice was more than cursory. It did not dissuade me from doing what I thought was right in the interests of my client.

In fact, prior to my retention by the public defender's

office in the Twentieth Judicial Circuit, the percentage of misdemeanor cases that went to trial in Judge Adam's court room was well under 25% (percent). It started slowly at first, but the more my reputation spread throughout the courthouse, jail and community, court dates jumped to three months out. By the time I had finished my first year, nearly every case on the docket proceeded to trial. Not because I wanted to take a trial in every case, but the tactics of the State Attorney's Office dictated it.

In trying to pressure me into submission, the policy of the state attorney's office changed. They refused to give any plea deals to my clients. Not even a standard one. I was new, committed and determined to do justice. I had no life outside the courthouse. I picked up the gauntlet. Soon, it appeared that playing golf on sultry afternoons or visiting the yacht club was becoming an issue for the judge, and the prosecutor was having to ask for extra help to keep up. Valuable resources of the State Attorney's' Office were getting stretched to the limit by a misdemeanor court room. Their new policy backfired.

Judge Adams and the assigned prosecutor in my courtroom, Assistant State's Attorney, Hamid Hunter, met with me in the Judge's office. He and the judge tried to persuade me to slow down. I was overwhelming the resources of their offices. The State had assigned several other attorneys from other dockets to assist Hamid Hunter in his efforts to prepare for trials and to assist with the mounting appeals' In their opinion, my overzealous efforts were unnecessary, and contrary to the public interest and those of my clients. I did not agree with their assessment. I balked at a system of justice that kept itself from collapse by forcing people to plea out to crimes that they did not commit or where the punishment felt unjust.

The judge had threatened to max out every sentence to the full extent of the law, should I lose at trial. I had to explain this pressure to each of my clients, on top of the rights and risks they already had in the dangers of losing. They could no longer expect the possibility of leniency. There would be no mitigating factors as provided to many other defendants. Nearly everyone I represented continued to have confidence in me. As long as I was willing to defend them, they wanted to go to trial. Surprisingly, even when I lost, clients were not sorry they did not plea. One wrote a letter from jail explaining that I was the first attorney who had ever 'fought' for him.

The parents of a young man accused of misdemeanor assault, who had watched attentively from the back of the courtroom, made an appointment to speak with me. The new charge became a violation of his felony probation once their son was found guilty. Although the minor assault charge only carried one year in the county jail, he was on probation for aggravated sexual battery. He was sent back to prison to finish his 25-year sentence, after I lost his misdemeanor trial.

The parents shuffled into my 6 x 8 office and sat down in the two chairs in front of my desk. My supervisor, Bea Taquachel, stood behind them. We were prepared to suffer their grievances. To our surprise, the parents thanked me. They lauded my performance at trial, and they shared how much their son was grateful for the efforts extended on his behalf.

A woman called later that month to thank me, still on probation for her criminal mischief charge. Another woman, whose daughter was facing a DUI charge came in to see me. Her daughter had failed to attend a mandatory court appearance, and an arrest warrant had been issued. She handed me a death certificate. My defendant, her daughter, had been run over by a drunk driver in the parking lot of a rock concert she had attended the night before her court date in Maimi. Despite her grief, she extended appreciation for her and her deceased daughter.

Several other defendants I represented wrote letters expressing their satisfaction with my representation, even the ones who pled. Others spoke to fellow prisoners who did it for them. Eventually, the sentient calls came in less frequently. The tide had changed. I began winning.

Judge Adams had developed a nervous tick. His lower jaw twitched before he read the verdict. Not guilty became a pattern. Over the next several months, it looked like he had developed TMJ. It wasn't long after my win-streak that the judge finally appealed to his old friend and boss, Bob Jacobs, the Public Defender. He moved me to Juvenile Court. I made an even bigger impression on Judge Carlin. Setting the bar higher made a difference.

Every attorney is different. Each are capable of doing amazing things. They set aside fear, as though it were a jacket. The yellow jacket of losing. The red jacket of embarrassment. The torn one that says I made so many mistakes I look like a fool. The aloof purple jacket that stands out, upsetting the apple cart. Of not being conformist and doing something creative. The green jacket of nausea, that fear of being badgered or chastised by the judge, superiors, or the prosecutor. Fear is the reason many attorneys never grow beyond that 1st year of experience.

I had a law partner once, a big bear of a man, over

six feet four inches tall and grizzled, with a square jaw and protruding forehead. Danny was intimidating to look at. He threw up and was violently ill before every trial call. He was so afraid of going to trial he literally 'forced' his clients to plea. Not by physically threatening them, but by scaring them. He would present the case in a manner that led them to believe they could not win and paint the worst sentence possible as the result. Even the seasoned defendant with many convictions behind him knew the risks and were willing to take it, regardless of the possible outcome, would not go to trial with Danny. Not because the case against them was great, but because they had no confidence in him. If Danny did not have trust in himself, how could anyone facing multiple years in prison?

Don't be alarmed. I was not unique, and Danny is not the norm. There are countless lawyers out there who love the law and care about their clients, more than job security or profits. Some value their integrity more than their precious license. They set their moral compass far above the minimal set of rules propounded by a professional organization that controls the behavior of copious member attorneys. So, never rule out the benefits of having an appointed attorney in lieu of a privately retained one until you've analyzed his or her credentials and abilities as outlined in this book.

Perhaps that large firm would be better than the smaller one. A public domain attorney may be equal to any private practicing attorney. The truth of the matter is, it's a coin toss. Public or private, large or small, is not determinative. It may well be worth considering the quality of the education by renowned institutions or the number of years of experience. But it is not a fool proof way to get the best attorney. Not a single attorney worth his salt could guarantee the result of their efforts on your behalf, even if they had won a favorable result for every person who walked into their office ahead of you. NONE.

The better attorney in any case is not found by looking at how much he charges, or whether she works in a large or smaller firm. It cannot be determined by how much they charge. Though a lot can be said about someone who, in public service, dedicates their best efforts tirelessly on behalf of her clients. However, like any other firm that employs many attorneys, at varying levels of experience and expertise, you could be assigned a good lawyer or one not as good. The real issue is how we define good where even the best may lose or win depending on variables outside of their control.

Although salient, these criteria should not be the only references used in evaluating your choice of a legal representative. Several factors that are worth considering in hiring an attorney are:

Education, from a reputable accredited university. There are some law schools that have not been accredited and as such graduates may be limited to only working in the jurisdiction the university or college is situated.

Specialization. Do they have any specialties, and is one in the area of law particular to your case?

Experience, how many years have they practiced, and in the particular area of law covering your need.

Honesty: aren't they all? Generally, lawyers are screened prior to becoming attorneys who can represent clients and even prior to entering law school.

None can have a felony on his record, or a misdemeanor if it concerns a crime of moral turpitude. One that attests to character, truthfulness and trustworthiness. Checking with the bar may give you some insight into whether they have been disciplined but that means relying on a potentially charged political organization to make your assessment. It may be worth noting but you give it the weight it deserves. Where there is power, there is potential for abuse.

Integrity, are they loyal to your case and will they see it through even if at a detriment to their own interests?

And most importantly, **Tenacity.** Will they leave no *viable* stone unturned to seek justice. Often stated as *zealous representation.*

CHAPTER TEN -

Transactional law. Contracts

Transactional law concerns, among other things, the drafting and interpretation of legal documents. If done correctly, you will not likely need to hire a litigation attorney to represent you in these proceedings.

The retainer, whether in a criminal or in a civil matter, outlines the agreement to pay the lawyer you hire for his or her legal services. A contract is a transaction between you and the lawyer. It is a writing setting out the parameters of each party's performance. He will likely remind you that it is a legally binding agreement and you should read it carefully and even get another lawyer to review it. Because most people will not likely pay a lawyer to review this agreement, the bar in most states require a "client bill of rights" explaining the duties required of the client and what the attorney responsibilities are. It also explains what to do in the event the client feels an injustice has been committed by the attorney. The Bar itself holds the attorney accountable for the proper administration of his duties. This makes the standard of performance much higher for the attorney because of his legal background and knowledge.

If you bought a household appliance or an automobile, you signed documents, a bill of sale or a promissory Note, certain tax forms, registration and title documents, or an installment contract. Real property, like a house, requires many documents that are drafted and interpreted by lawyers. People trained in transactional language or laws draft these documents that if done correctly, keep most matters out of court or in the event there is a disagreement, it works to protect the rights of the client that the paperwork was intended for. Generally, that client is not you but the individual, firm or corporation, that originally requested the documents to be created.

The Bar and legislatures in most states have taken additional measures to ensure that consumers' interests are protected. Consumer protection regulations such as the "Lemon" laws are enacted to protect consumers against unscrupulous business practices. Real property has even stricter regulations and the Bar becomes involved, similar to a quasi-governmental regulatory agency. It sets up and oversees professional standards and usually approves the contract and other forms used in transactions. It sets certain educational requirements for licensed real estate brokers and agents. Generally, a person does not retain an attorney to draft an agreement to protect their interests in real property transactions. These contracts would likely be similar and are standardized in most instances. Buyers are encouraged to have an attorney to read over the documents (transactions) or hire one if disagreements need to be litigated.

A transactional lawyer may be the estate agent who drafted your grandfather's Will or trust or other estate documents that you may be the beneficiary. He may or may not be the probate attorney you hire to file the documents or litigate matters that become contested. Transactions and litigation require different skills and experience. The focus and goal of one is not always aligned with the other. Knowing the difference between each ensures that one can have confidence they hired the right attorney to successfully meet their needs in the matter at hand. Getting a Massy-Ferguson mechanic to fix your Toyota may work out alright but it sure gives the driver that assurance she needs to traverse those long-distance trips to grandma's house, if the mechanic is trained or experienced in repairing your make of car, without additional anxiety.

CHAPTER ELEVEN -

The Boutique law firm

Stringer, although his intentions are good, is simply naïve to think one lawyer can do it all. True, there are some firms or attorneys who handle more than one type of law, and are willing to take on your matters, say in criminal and family law, but it's a rare lawyer who knows every kind of law well enough to not make a mistake. That is likely why the percentage of general practitioners in law is low. In fact, the ones who usually 'do it all' admit it is not something they want to do but are compelled to try by circumstance or other considerations.

In states like South Dakota and Idaho, and the Virgin Islands, the bar exam pass rates are high. Twenty or more years ago, they were nearly 100 percent. There was such a need for legal professionals that special rules were created allowing paralegals and other trained individuals to assist people with their legal matters in and out of court.

In some specialties like Patent Law, additional qualifications in education exist for one to practice. Most jurisdictions require an engineering degree as well as a J.D. to be admitted to practice. In International Law, Education Law, and Administrative Law, or subjects concerning international treaties or intellectual property, and copyright infringements, few lawyers are knowledgeable. It simply is not lucrative enough or requires too much time and effort to familiarize oneself with the varied procedures and rules that dissuade many from entering, unless totally immersed in these fields.

Where there are shortages of trained professionals, some lawyers will attempt to assist a client. These attorneys are at risk of having bar complaints filed or sued by the same clients they endeavored to help. Nonetheless, they do it. Most of the time the courts see it as a needed public service in the community and are more patient and tolerant. However, there is a chance they will not give someone a break. Some courts may find the attorney in contempt of court or may recommend them to the bar's disciplinary committee for discipline.

Early into my private practice, two young mothers came into my office after visiting several other firms and attorneys in a desperate attempt to get someone to sue the Lee County School Board. A public entity with an 800-million-dollar budget. The mothers had only $2,500 between them for costs. I balked, too.

The cause of action was a violation of Florida's Sunshine Act. The remedy limited by the statute was merely to force the board to disclose the error and redo the regulatory ruling, in the "Sunshine", before a hearing open to the public. There were no monitory damages. No money to be made except a provision for the recovery of attorney fees and costs---for the prevailing side. Recall that law is a business. It's profit driven. A lot of time and effort would likely be donated on behalf of a cause, and possibly a lost one, at best.

After listening to Liz M. and Gail B., I empathized with them as single parents. The school board had changed the school start times during a closed-door session. Buses would pick up elementary school children before the sun came up. These working-class mothers argued that their six-year-old children would be standing on dark street corners waiting for a bus in high crime neighborhoods without supervision. The older teens would get out of school much later and miss work. These young workers serve and bus tables in restaurants or perform other ministerial but necessary duties in the community. The change to school start times impacted, not just the parents and students, but the entire community. They would have to adapt their businesses accordingly. The sudden disruption would cost businesses thousands of dollars.

The young mothers had a video tape recording showing the chairman of the school board, admitting to having "secret meetings" when they made this "ministerial" change. At that time my practice was mostly criminal and family law, and some personal injury. I knew nothing about Education Law. I had some basic exposure to Constitutional law while in the Office of the Public Defender. The mothers were outraged by the elected officials flagrant disregard of parents' rights and safety for their children. I reluctantly accepted the case, hoping to familiarize myself with the particulars of the law and the proceedings necessary to prosecute it.

The mothers came up with a name that would be certain to garner the attention of the court and media; Parents and Students for Safe, Sensible, School, Start Times (PSSSSST v. Lee County School Board). We filed it in federal court, not state court, my first mistake—or perhaps not.

In one of my first trials before, the Honorable Judge Adams, in county court, as a transplanted Yankee, I was nearly found in contempt. I made a *faux pas* during closing argument. I was representing a former Marine charged with a DUI. He was arrested twenty feet from his driveway after he supposedly failed the sobriety test and admitted that: 'at some point several hours earlier in the day [he] had a beer.'

I attempted to express my client's outrage, without using the colorful language he had used in my office at our first meeting. Hamid Hunter, the prosecutor in the case, found something I had said offensive. He objected.

"Sustained." Judge Adams looked at me sternly and shook his head. I had no idea what was objectionable. Each time I asked, he'd say: "You know. I don't have to repeat it."

I tried restating my closing a different way. Without Hamid's objection, the judge sustained it again. I was utterly perplexed. I looked up at the bench flustered and asked:

"What did I say?"

He looked even more cross and chastised me for using profanity in his court room. The jury looked amused. I started my final argument again apparently repeating the offensive word.

"Objection!" Hamid Hunter jumped up out of his seat in a show of outrage. "Judge, she said it again."

Still stumped I asked the court, "What word does he find offensive?"

"You know. I should not have to repeat it." Unlike the jury, Judge Adams was not smiling.

After another attempt to give my closing argument, and a jumping objection, the judge called us both up to his bench. This time he threatened to find me in contempt of court if I used that word again.

"What word?!" I was worried but thoroughly confounded.

"You really don't know?" Hamid was amused. Apparently, "a Southern lady would never use the word: "Pissed". It's nasty." he said.

I was in the heart of Old Dixie. A statue of General Robert E. Lee—the namesake of the county the court was situated—sat atop a granite horse across the street from the federal courthouse. Southern tradition was still upheld. The manners and roles of men and women were biblically enforced if not by the law, then by the men and women who served it. PSSSSST was suggestive enough to create controversy. Immediately upon receipt of the documents filed in the case, the Clerk redacted the plaintiff's name with a colored pencil, drawing the press to inquire further.

Reporters from all over the county greeted the two young mothers and I on the granite steps of the federal courthouse. Cameras pointed in our direction as we came out. Judge Steele had dismissed the mother's case. He sent it down to the state court to decide, citing his reason as: "matters traditionally controlled by state law"—like ministerial acts of school boards. He didn't chastise me. He didn't reprimand me. He didn't sanction me for wasting the court's time. He just smiled wide for the cameras.

The risks taken by general practitioners are innumerable. It was an unfamiliar area of law. I nearly bungled the case by filing it in the wrong court. It lacked jurisdiction, or so it claimed. I could have been found in contempt of court, fined, and sent to the regulatory branch of the state bar, but Judge Steele gave me a break. Albeit only after he heard arguments and garnered substantial publicity. His photo ran alongside of ours, on the front page of the Garnett owned newspaper: "Newpress." The largest afternoon daily newspaper in Southwest Florida at the time.

Reporters from several national media groups including major television networks and local news stations, had interviewed us on the courthouse steps in downtown Fort Myers. Two local mothers taking on a mega-budget School Board made national news. Someone told me that anytime someone got above the fold in a newspaper it was worth $60,000 in advertising alone. But it could have ended badly for the young mothers, and I, as an inexperienced attorney.

A lesson learned why most attorneys are reluctant to practice outside of a few specialty areas.

PART III
THE MACHINERY

CHAPTER TWELVE -

The Nuts and Bolts in Hiring a Lawyer

Almost every book you buy on how to hire an attorney are filled with legal jargon and cite a few instances of angst for those who venture it alone. It reiterates several rules and regulations showing how the practice of law is highly regulated and specialized. The questions they suggest, although phrased in varying ways, stress the same things: education, specialization, experience and honesty—as cast in the form of disciplinary records with the bar. It is as though there is some conspiracy out there, leading you to the same conclusion. *Any attorney who meets the established criteria can represent you.* Yes, but is this helpful?

As stated, all these things may be important to consider, but it does nothing to answer your question: How to hire a lawyer? What's implied in your question is as important as what is stated. It's like going pearl diving in Boston Harbor. Are there a lot of clams? Maybe, but are there any *pearls* likely to be in them. Rare, but possible. But as those other books imply, the one you want is among them. Happy clamming! Will you need waders?

No, that won't be necessary. Here is where the circus separates the clowns from the barkers, and the trapeze artists from the knife throwers. Follow along with the scenario I painted for you in the introduction, so you can visualize the kind of lawyer you want working on your matter.

The brightest pearls – persnickety, tenacity, and hutzpah!

In each anecdote I am certain you perceived there were traits that were notable. These remarkable characteristics are what you should be looking for in *your* inquiry for a lawyer. Absent affordability and reputation, the latter we will examine in more detail, are personal to the individual. Interestingly, these traits are the same qualities that make one a good leader. They are articulate, creative, candid, tenacious, fearless, and prideful without being arrogant. These are the nuts and the bolts of good legal representation. The pearl among sow's ears!

Notice I left knowledge and honesty out of the list. To get through law school and pass a bar exam, one had to be reasonably free of moral turpitude, not have an austere criminal record and be somewhat intelligent. Although, some might beg to differ, we need not waste time trying to figure out whether he or she is an idiot.

Let's start with the most pressing issue that threatens your freedom.

CHAPTER THIRTEEN –

The Lynchpin in finding the Right Lawyer

We have covered this subject in the previous chapters and demonstrated a need for a lawyer when emotions could cloud judgment, or when your freedom and future employment status are at stake. Whether you choose private representation or public representation will depend on your financial condition. If modest savings and income as assumed in this scenario, you will likely have an appointed counsel from one of the public offices available. Appointed is not retained. You did not hire this lawyer. It was given to you by the court. You can keep her or release her and hire your own lawyer.

In the earlier chapters we discussed a method of determining whether she is the attorney you want representing you in court. Perhaps she has the qualities you find necessary to serve your interests. The purpose of the anecdote in the previous sections was to reveal insights into how some lawyers think. This is not like how a motor works or how a clock ticks but how each performs under conditions unique to your needs. Think of it as being a necessity to suit your job as a lighthouse operator as opposed to a janitor. Is the accuracy of a chronometer necessary to protect shipwrecks or is a simple watch or the clock on your phone sufficient, if all you do is use it to get to your next cleaning assignment on time.

Say you are the LAN specialists that must synchronize thousands of computers in cities around the world precisely when other technicians are standing by, as opposed to the IT Guy, who sits quietly in the corner office waiting for you to reset that password you forgot. The purpose of hiring a lawyer of your choice is to meet your specific goals.

If you are an Uber driver making a few dollars to supplement your income, perhaps any attorney would be able to answer some basic questions and advise you. I mean, they went to law school, passed the bar exam, and are a member of a state bar governing their behavior. However, it may be more necessary if you own a taxi business, a medallion, or are a delivery driver making a living on your license.

A DUI, has significant ramifications for professional drivers like over the road (OTR) truck drivers. Police officers, security specialists, and bus drivers. Any criminal infraction, no matter how small, may affect your future employment. Sometimes even a simple speeding ticket could change your future employability.

When I enlisted into the United States Armed Forces in 1976, I was selected to work for an agency of the government I and most Americans at the time, had never heard of—the National Security Agency (NSA). After nearly two years of specialized training, at a cost to the taxpayers of $250,000 the secretive organization operationally controlled my every move, while wearing a uniform and being paid by the US Airforce.

One of the requisites of being selected was that I had to have a clean record. No civil infractions or criminal record. Not even a ticket for littering. The records of its candidates had to be squeaky clean. I underwent a thorough special background investigation (SBI) conducted by the FBI. I had no civil or criminal record that might make me susceptible to blackmail by enemy agents, i.e., usually the KGB of the former Soviet Union. After training and expenditure, we had to be careful, not to arouse suspicion even from a mere traffic violation. Anything in the public records would give away our location and other personal information that could be used against us in the event we were shot down and captured. If I failed, I could be reassigned to a missile silo somewhere in North Dakota as a cook. Thus, one simple DUI would have changed my future. It may or may not be that way today for government analysts for the NSA but if you are or intend to hold a security clearance, be prepared. Hitsuzen is a bitch!

If I was in your shoes, I would want to hire an attorney with the qualities outlined earlier simply because I want the best attorney for my future, especially where it is yet undetermined. I never knew when I passed a series of tests during basic training that I would qualify for a special job that set the course of my entire future. The young seldom look beyond the horizon. Having a squeaky-clean record gave me opportunities I never would have had. But how do you find someone who meets those criteria, when all of them are purported to be highly trained, honest, zealous representatives, you ask?

It all depends on only one criterion. The lynchpin that binds all the valuable traits together under one criteria. Imagine that! Just one item on your shopping list to hire the perfect lawyer for your case—Reputation.

CHAPTER FOURTEEN –

Reputation—the emperor's new clothes

My father once told me that it takes thirty years to build a good reputation and 30 seconds to destroy it.

Michael Jackson was at the top of his career and had a reputation as one of the most popular musicians in the world, prior to being accused of child molestation. O.J. Simpson, the legendary Running Back with the Buffalo Bills football team, set records and won more titles than any similar player at the time. His reputation as a great athlete became superseded by his reputation as someone who got away with murder and paid for it—civilly. Richard Milhouse Nixon was one of the most popular US presidents in the early 70's. He won the 1972 election with 49 out of 50 states securing 520 electoral votes and 60.7% of the popular vote. Two years into office, after his landslide victory over Geroge McGovern, came the Watergate scandal and his eventual resignation from public office. He upended his good reputation to become infamous. A villain not a 'crook'. He was pardoned by his successor, Gerald Ford, before he was even convicted.

One did not have to go too far or ask too many questions to find out the reputations of these notable celebrities. It was widely published in the media. One could tell, simply by listening to Michael Jackson's songs on the radio or watching O.J. rush down a field on Monday Nights or watch the historic events of Nixon's rise and fall unfold in their living rooms in the 1970s. What their reputations were, the good and bad, was determined by the viewers, the fans, critics and public in general. But how do you find the reputations of attorneys who are almost invisible, professionals not in the limelight? Interestingly, each has a reputation too, just not as widely known as a celebrity.

There once was a promising young attorney in the public defender's office when I was there, in early 1999. Sebastian was young, handsome and pretty well off. He had a trust fund. He didn't need the job and people wondered why he was starting his career in the basement of the legal community. In a short time, he had built a reputation of being brilliant in his analysis of a case and articulate in his closing argument. He won cases even when the evidence was against his client. His reputation as a brilliant and winning attorney carried him into private practice. It wasn't long after he started in the private sector, he was unobtainable. Few but the very wealthy could afford his services. He had a whirlwind career. Or so, everyone thought. Ten years later, someone told me he had hung himself in a jail cell after being arrested on multiple felony charges. He got into hard drugs and in a flash, his career was gone. With his trust fund attached and reputation diminished, he was finished—on the verge of being disbarred. The life of one of Florida's most gifted young attorneys snuffed out before he reached the age of 45.

Many promising young lawyers become obscure and forgotten names in a matter of years. How many people remember Douglas Schmidt, the lawyer for Dan White who shot San Francisco Supervisor, Harvey Milk, in 1978?

Perhaps the diminished capacity argument Schmidt made might jog your memory—ever heard of the Twinkie defense? Or F. Lee Bailey, and the famed 'Palimony' suit that garnered national attention when Actor Lee Marvin lost a large sum of his estate by his long-time gal-pal (domestic partner). Bailey argued an alternative recovery similar to the legal alimony that married women receive after a divorce. Their fame, or reputation as it is, came from handling one important, high-profile case. Or, in the case of a few attorneys like Alan Dershowitz, several.

Who remembers OJ's Dream Team? Besides Dershowitz, who were the other attorneys? How were they popular in their respective jurisdictions? Each member had areas of specialty unique to their own styles. Johnny Cochran had already garnered national attention for his flamboyant showmanship. His uncanny ability to create phrases like: "If the glove doesn't fit, you must acquit" contributed to the not guilty verdict in OJ's high-profile case.

Without going into further detail, these attorneys' reputations flourished and had one thing in common, creativity. The ability to think outside the box. All the dream team defense needed to do was chip away at reasonable doubt. The prosecution and the police presented multiple opportunities for them to exercise their craftsmanship. Their over-zealous hurried investigation made them vulnerable. It became a circus. The audience and jury—were amused and fascinated—before being appalled. But what made it *extra* incredible was the reputation of each performer. These men earned their reputations. In trial after trial, they practiced their craft and honed their skills until they got it right. Before they even came into that California court room in 1995, people knew they were good attorneys. Skilled at what they do. It was their reputation for being smart and creative, that extra bit of credibility, that gave them the edge.

Reputation can be a reversible jacket, famous or infamous but it's no less quintessential. My son-in-law, Jim, is a diehard Buccaneer fan. He was not fond of the Patriots great quarterback, Tom Brady--until he came to play for Tampa. His perception changed almost overnight. As though he put on a pair of rose-colored sunglasses and everything including, the 'biggest cheater ever to play football', began to look rosy.

Reputation is elusive. It's illusive. Like an invisible cloak. It's the one thing you wear that you never exclusively own. The public owns it, and you are allowed to wear it so long as you don't get it dirty. It's a precious prize you receive and not something you buy, nor inherit. You earn it, but there's no guarantee you get to keep it. Nonetheless, reputation is the one essential thing you can count on when you want to hire a lawyer. The right lawyer for your case.

Reputation is more than the number of years of experience someone has in a job or field of study. A lawyer could practice law for twelve years and have only one year of experience–repeated a dozen times. It is what is earned by experience and practice and not the mere passing of time. What's earned is the good reputation people see. How good the value—depends on how you are seen by others. That buzz in the courthouse whenever someone brings up your name.

"Where's Michelle?" someone would ask, and everyone within earshot would say, almost in unison: "She's in trial!"

My reputation as a fighter grew rapidly. Within one year out of the public defender's office and into private practice, I had more cases as a solo practitioner than many firms with multiple attorneys. In the year the Clerk's office became automated and upgraded to a computerized system, the clerk of court had not envisioned any firm or attorney carrying as many active cases as I had. They had to keep some manually on the books as I had already exceeded the capacity of the system before it went into operation.

There was simply no time available in a single day to get everything done but somehow my young office managed to stay afloat. Almost every day I had a trial call in one of the court rooms before multiple judges who had to coordinate with each other to move their docket. My reputation as a busy attorney only contributed to further inquiries as to: why? People wondered: How could a junior attorney (someone practicing less than 4 years) be getting so many cases and trials?

The short answer is reputation.

Besides being appointed to multiple complex cases by the bench, referrals began unexpectedly coming from many judicial offices, as well as opposing counsel and inmates. Inmates boasted and compared a letter showing me appointed in their case as winning the lottery. A beloved senior judge, Thompson, labeled me the 'Patron Saint of Impossible Cases' after appointing me to several capital sex felonies to defend.

One of the toughest judges on the bench in Lee County at the time—known as "No Release" Reese—a former army colonel, chastised a defendant charged in a

First-degree Felony Hit and Run case. He appeared before his bench without counsel at a Docket Sounding. Upon further inquiry, the defendant admitted I fired him for lying to me. My motion to withdraw was filed earlier and I was in trial in another courtroom on another matter. Judge Reese continued the defendant's trial for one week. The judge strongly recommended that he return to my office and beg me to take him back as a client.

Reputation sometimes grows like a weed in the shadows and not always in the sunshine. Many judges are appointed by the governor and recommended by judicial committees. Most must thereafter be elected and are thus political in nature. They are influenced by things noted in the community media. They make mental notes of cases they see that garner the public's attention. Cases like 'Dog' Tracy, who was charged with a public nuisance for having 35 dogs in his three-bedroom home in a residential community. The case of a young boy run over in a drug deal by another young man whose family raised a national cry for justice.

Ralph Looseman looked a lot like a young Harry Potter at the height of the series' popularity. Putting him in a pullover sweater and round wireframe glasses confirmed it. When his case was dismissed after a motion before a Charlotte County judge. The media and family appeared outraged that he got away with murder. Or as in the PSSSST case that also made national news. Two young single mothers taking on a high-budget multi-district school board. These sensational cases aside, what really impresses the bench are the more sophisticated trials that reveal technical proficiency.

One of my first felony cases in private practice was with a young black defendant who, unable to pay the bond, remained incarcerated in the Lee County jail for more than 2 years. He was charged with aggravated battery on his two-year-old son. A witness saw him callously throw his young son into the back seat. The state claimed it caused a hematoma (brain-bleed) that led to severe mental retardation. The defendant had fired all previously appointed attorneys who wanted him to plea. The judge who appointed me, knew my reputation for taking difficult cases to trial. And based on the reputation I had built in the Public Defender's office, the State Attorney assigned Francine Donarummo, his chief prosecutor, to try the case.

On re-cross of the toddler victim's mother—high risk even in a less emotionally charged case—I revealed that she had dropped the child on his head while the boy was still in his car seat, a week prior to letting the baby's daddy have his visitation. When asked why she had not informed us on direct and cross examination, the young mother looked over at Francine, the state's star prosecutor and pointed—"She told me not to." This was blatant attorney misconduct. Interfering with a witness's testimony is a felony, but the judge and I chose to ignore it. No need to report it to the bar, when the State Attorney himself now had a record to frame the appropriate punishment for one of his most zealous assistants—Francine was his division chief.

My expert, a Punta Gorda neurosurgeon, that I had coaxed out of retirement, suffered from prostate cancer. He testified, in obvious discomfort, that a hematoma like this one could have been formed nearly a month earlier depending on how fast the bleed. The state attorney's expert, a young pediatrician with only one neuro case in her history, was unable to refute that claim. My defendant, Cederick Lee, was 21 at the time of the incident. I was appointed on his 22nd birthday. By the time the jury deliberated and came back with a not guilty verdict, he was one week away from his 23rd birthday. Cederick had spent nearly 2 years in the Lee County Jail refusing all plea offers that would have freed him but would have severed his parental rights. Francine refused to shake hands as was customary for opposing counsel after a trial. She ran out of the courtroom after the verdict was read, presumably in tears.

She had done everything right according to the textbook. Even caught a break when I left a local attorney on the jury. A risky move, but worth it not to have a lesser charge available for the jury to compromise. They may have felt less resolute where a child may have been irreparably harmed in the defendant's custody. I had hoped and later learned after speaking with the attorney-juror, Mike Fink, who was made foreman, that the jury was wafting. They wanted the lesser charge of neglect, thinking that someone had to pay for the crime. Mike explained to them the standard of reasonable doubt and the duty a jury had to uphold the constitutional precept of presumption of innocence. If there was any doubt he the one who hurt the child, the lesser crime would also be unavailable.

I was the buzz of the courthouse that week. The State Attorney's Office had taken the video recording of my "Raincoat" voir dire, on building a reasonable doubt, and made it a training video for its new attorneys. However, reputation is more than one or two interesting cases. It is a stacked selection of experiences and challenges overcome to earn respect in a community. It's akin to the construction of a house, built from the foundation up, one brick at a time.

CHAPTER FIFTEEN –

A Double-Edged Sword

At another case in Collier County, I represented a Cuban immigrant and his son charged with felony trafficking in narcotics. He and his 20-year-old son were separated for trial. I represented the primary defendant, the father. Another local attorney was appointed to the son's case. Carlos (not his real name) made his living as a painter, working as a crewmember on new construction around the Collier County area.

In Cuba he had been a member of the military. He fled the country several years earlier with three other soldiers in a small dingy. They set out from Cuba hoping to make the 90-mile trek to Florida but were intercepted by the U.S. Coast Guard. He spent time in a Miami compound with numerous other illegal aliens awaiting disposition. After his plea for asylum was accepted, he moved to Naples, and got a job painting houses in the mushrooming construction market of the 1990's. He saved money and eventually hired someone to get his son out of Cuba, but his wife refused to leave.

For more than three years he and his son lived and worked in Southwest Florida making a good living as painters and did not commit any crimes. One day a newly hired painter, another Hispanic man, approached him and asked him if he knew where he could score some cocaine. Carlos said he did not, but the man pressed him daily claiming he was desperate because his family were in jeopardy and needed money soon. After several attempts by the man to get Carlos to help him, he yielded. He had met many unsavory people in the Miami compound while he was in custody and agreed to contact one who he knew to be part of an organized criminal ring.

The man who Carlos thought of as a friend after several months of working with him, was an informant with long criminal history. After being caught again he had made a plea deal with the State of Florida to work off some time—5 years for every criminal brought to justice. His sentence was over 25 years per conviction and he had several. His plea arrangement required he provide a certain number of felony arrests as incentive to reduce his prison sentence. The informant had to get Carlos to procure a large cache of drugs and set him up to meet an undercover agent posing as a buyer at a prearranged location in Collier County.

Oh, entrapment you say to yourself. What's the big deal?

The entrapment defense had not been successfully done in Florida for more than ten years prior to my decision to use this defense. Juries are reluctant to let an otherwise good citizen go where they admitted to a crime. Because of this waiver of the right not to self-incriminate, the court usually conducts a hearing prior to the use of the defense. Particularly where it is often a wolf in a sheep suit, more akin to jury nullification, than a real defense.

Ideally, if the state enticed someone to commit a crime where he did not have the propensity to commit such a crime but for the state's enticement, they would nullify the crime by letting the defendant go free. It appeals to the sense of fairness that every citizen has a right to feel from its government incrimination.

There are two types of entrapment, subjective and objective. Subjective considers the propensity of the defendant, the latter requires egregious conduct by the police or some planned scheme that shocks the conscience of right-minded people. Kind of like, erecting a state sponsored meth lab down the street from an elementary school in order to entice bad guys to commit a crime. Taxpayers and parents really don't favor this method or crime fighting.

The likelihood of the success of this active defense heavily rests on the facts of a case. If an individual was a drug addict for example and was found in possession of drugs, it would not be wise to argue he was entrapped by the state, where he had a propensity to use drugs and thus possessed them. Not that he couldn't, but it's imprudent in most cases. The defense requires the defendant to make an admission to the crime. He is excused (some say nullified) by the jury if they believe he was unreasonably enticed by the police to commit the crime. However, where the idea of the crime originates with a state actor, and the defendant was someone who never used drugs, or had no criminal history, the defense is stronger. Carlos had no propensity to commit the crime but for the state enticing him, several times, before he relinquished and agreed to procure the illegal drugs. Juries are alarmed when they think the government is manufacturing crimes to make criminals, but it requires the defendant to persuade them first that he was not inclined to commit a crime but for the state's actions.

Judges often gather at closed meetings and social gatherings as well as educational seminars and official functions. They share stories about interesting cases or challenging attorneys they had to contend with over time. They even call each other occasionally to make inquiries or discuss dockets and how to effectively move them. Names come up. I imagine mine came up more than a few times as the number of trials and successes escalated.

My reputation for tenacity and innovative defenses had soared like a hot air balloon on fire throughout the state. It filled the court room on the day of trial. All seats were taken by a slew of unfamiliar faces. Legal professionals and State's attorneys, assistants, staff, and curiosity seekers from every corner of the state looking at what could be the resurgence of a formidable defense. The state of Florida and not the Twentieth Judicial District took over the prosecution of the case. If they would quash the rise of entrapment at its reemergence, they would have a double victory. They had assigned one of its leading prosecutors and an assistant from the Florida Department of Law Enforcement (FDLE) with ties to the jurisdiction, the daughter in law of my favorite Fort Myers arbiter, Judge Thompson.

Not having had an opportunity to depose the informant prior to trial, partially due to the protections afforded confidential informants, the judge upon granting my motion allowed me to depose him at a break the morning before commencement of the state's case. I would not have a transcript, just the few notes I scribbled on a pad. It was enough for me to know how to proceed on cross-examination. He was a three-time felon with a deep want and desire to remain out of prison. He had a written agreement with the state to provide a number of years off his sentence for every successful criminal prosecution he assisted with.

A sound and desperate reason to entice to my client to help him 'get money to help his family' by committing to get drugs from a former criminal contact Carlos had met at the INS detention center in Miami.

In my opening argument I feigned a terrible Spanish accent portraying my client telling the story of his bold escape from Communist Cuba in a dingy with two other soldiers. How he left his wife and newborn son to come to America to start a new life in the land of the free and work for several years to save enough money as a painter, to bring his family to him. Two Hispanic jurors, a young man and a middle-aged woman both had tears in their eyes before I was through. By the time the state put on its confidential informant witness, the jury had already formed an opinion. They suspected from my opening admission, my defendant had committed the crime, to help a man trying desperately to help his family, like he did his own.

The Not Guilty verdict that followed the end of a three-day trial had silenced the court room full of law enforcement officials and prosecutors. Subjective Entrapment as a defense was back! The jury had found Carlos guilty on lesser charges of minor possession and sentenced him to probation. To Carlos, and later his son, where his attorney used much of my case to bolster his success, and to the public, who believed in our system of justice—I was a hero. I showed the law worked not just in favor of the rich and powerful, but to the working-class man, single working mothers, school children unlawfully detained, and many down and out folk with limited opportunities. Those who struggled to survive on the very streets that led to the courthouse.

I fought a perverted system of justice, where bad guys could make otherwise good men go bad, to lessen their sentences. In cases that followed, I was in the media regularly. From defending a Doctor's son charged with homicide after a school fight ended badly, to two average men arrested for DUI by the city of Cape Coral attempting to train their police-officers at mobile check-points, a charming Cuban hitman for the Cartel, the "Pillowcase Bandit" who made his living burglarizing wealthy residences for the Mafia, and an Alabama family trying desperately to get the remains of a loved one back from the husband who murdered her before he could cremate the body. On Court-TV, Nancy Grace had called me out wondering: "Who is this lovely lady in lavender."

Then, there was Arthur Lee Coleman, Jr. Killed by law enforcement while he was working as an informant. I had successfully defended Art in a Second-Degree Homicide and assisted in placing him with police to assist with their investigation into organized crime. He wanted to dispose of several other felony cases the police had charged him with besides the murder.

The U.S. Marshall's task force, made up of mostly local law enforcement from the Lee County Sheriff's Office, surrounded a home in a Fort Myers residential area in the wee hours of the morning. A ping from a cell phone indicated his location to within a 100 feet—where houses were stacked much closer. While talking to the owner of the house, the mother of one of Art's former girlfriends, they saw an SUV backing out of a garage next door, and in a flash of gunfire halted the driver before he exited the driveway.

Fortunately, for them the dead black man with his

brains blown out behind the wheel happened to be Art, and not some poor schmuck going to work early. Representing the family, I sued the Sheriff, several of his deputies, and the U.S. Marshall's Office in federal court for wrongful death and violations of Art's civil rights. They were serving a warrant for violation of his probation. A probation that was a façade, created to give him credibility and hide his part as an informant. Doug Sprotte, the State Attorney who promised to keep an eye out for any warrant for violations, was on vacation in the Virgin Islands.

These cases bolstered my reputation and papered my career. Stories that fell above and below the fold in the front and inner pages of newspapers and magazines and I was interviewed on television for nearly ten years before my reputation eventually drew the attention of the conservative system that I was threatening. Every trial, appeal and overturned conviction changes the law subtly, and at times not so subtly. To some, I had become the antithesis Hygeia wrote about.

If reputation was a balloon, mine had blown up into a Zephyr, the Goodyear Blimp—flying high over the Superbowl above the cheering crowds. It wouldn't develop into the Hindenburg until several years later, when it came crashing down, after the bar fallaciously prosecuted me on ethical violations.

On September 4, 2004, four years after I had been admitted to the Florida bar, a document left my office "ON MY LETTERHEAD" that the Florida bar claimed was a false subpoena. Seven years and two cases later, they suspended me for 91 days. It took them seven years. Seven years of high-profile cases in the media and continued confidence by the public to hire a lawyer, with my distinguished and depreciating reputation.

CONCLUSION.

Reputation is perception. How often have we seen in the news over the past few years many popular celebrities and politicians fade into oblivion or go down in flames for one moment of bad judgment. Even when the report is made up or proven false later, the lingering odor of ash remains. Nonetheless, reputation, good or bad, is the lynch pin that holds the answer to your question, how to hire a lawyer, or *kill* one (figuratively), if you decide not to hire based on the negative side of the topic.

The method is simple, call an attorney in the specialty you need, and ask him or her to provide references, or call other attorneys or people you know in an area to inquire what they have heard about the attorney. Research the matter online, or in the papers, periodicals, or other media. If the matter is criminal, the best resources are available, but behind the bars of a county jail may not be accessible to you, unless you know someone on the inside. However, bail bondsmen, police officers, court clerks or employees are easily accessible, and I have found they are often happy to provide their opinion as to who is the best or worst at whatever job you need.

If the matter is civil, like transactional or probate, look to courthouse employees, bankers, tax accountants, financial planners, and funeral parlor managers who may provide good sources. Civil rights attorneys or lawyers who sue governments and officials are rare. You can call or contact the state bar directly for a list. Personal injury attorneys are advertising in every forum, but to find the better one for you, simply call any firm and ask for their referral list, then compare notes when you call them to inquire. If you have the time, sit in on some public matters in the courthouse and inquire among the attorneys and other professionals and staff. Most if not all, would provide some enlightenment.

Happy hunting!

#

BIBLIOGRAPHY

1. https:/www.michbar.org//file/public_resources/hirelawyer.pdf; A Practical Guide to Hiring a Lawyer

2. https:/www.media.floridabar.org/uploads/2026/04; Florida Rules of Civil Procedure

3. https:/floridabar.org/ florida bar rules of professional conduct - Search

4. Lawless, Joseph F., 4th Ed., Professional Misconduct, 2024 cumulative supplement, LexisNexis, Michie (2024)

5. Prosser, William L., Keeton, W.P., Prosser and Keeton On Torts, 5th Ed., WEST GP, (1984)

6. Tammi S. Etheridge, *The Big Cost of Small Farms*, 77 Fla. L. Rev. 465 (2025).
   Available at: https://scholarship.law.ufl.edu/flr/vol77/iss2/3

7. Cook, Joseph G., Marcus, P., Criminal Law, 8th Ed., Carolina Academic Press (2024)

8. Denning, Lord Alfred, Landmarks in the Law, Oxford University Press (1984).

9. Dickens, Charles, Bleak House, reprint, Arcturus Publishing (2019)

10. Lee, Harper, To Kill A Mocking Bird, Harper, NY, (2025)

11. Harr, J., A Civil Action, Vintage (1996)

12. Ehrhardt, Audrey, How to Hire a Lawyer, Book Baby (2017)

13. Newton, J., The Client Centered Law Firm, Blue Check Publishing (2020)

14. IDM Law, Roche, M. (editor), Speak Like a Lawyer Write Like a Lawyer, Amazon (2024)

15. Brooks, Jennifer L.; Lordan, Christopher H.; Robinson, Michael P.; and Pandozzi, Neal R. (1999) "1998 Survey of Rhode Island Law: Cases: Criminal Procedure," *Roger Williams University Law Review*: Vol. 4: Iss. 2, Article 12. Available at: https://docs.rwu.edu/rwu_LR/vol4/iss2/12

16. Sheppard, Ann B. (2001) "2000 Survey of Rhode Island Law: Cases: Professional Conduct," *Roger Williams University Law Review*: Vol. 6: Iss. 2, Article 16.
Available at: https://docs.rwu.edu/rwu_LR/vol6/iss2/16

17. Bonilla, Alexus (2022) "DeCurtis v. Visconti, Boren & Campbell Ltd., 252 A.3d 765 (R.I. 2021)," Roger Williams University Law Review: Vol. 27: Iss. 3, Article 24. Available at: https://docs.rwu.edu/rwu_LR/vol27/iss3/24

18. Albert, R., How Constitutions Die, Vol. 77, Issue 4, 2025 | Published by Florida Law Review

19. **Fla. L. Rev.** Russell D. Covey, *Longitudinal Guilt:*

Repeat Offenders, Plea Bargaining, and the Variable Standard of Proof, 63 Fla. L. Rev. 431 (2011).

20. https://archives.naplesnews.com/news/crime/ Three shootings by Lee deputies raise question: Who is investigating?
21. https://www.police1.com/vehicle-incidents/articles/Fla. man shot, killed after hitting officer with car,
22. Dershowitz, Alan, The Devil's Advocate, Warner Books (1994)
23. Johns, C.H., The Code of Hammurabi, Arcani Press (2020)
24. Holmes, Oliver, W., Jr., The Common Law, Rev.Ed., Dover Press, (2013)
25. Plucknett, Theordore, F.T., The Concise History of the Common Law, First Ed., (Amazon/Kindle) Liberty Fund Inc. (2010)
26. https://www.floridalawreview.com/issue/12901-vol-77-issue-4-2025

ACKNOWLEDGMENTS

To my lord and savior, Jesus Christ, whom all things are possible. He granted me my miracle and has never left me through good times and bad. To Him, I owe everything, all that I was, am, and will ever be. To my family who stood behind me and never let me fall. To my friends who turned their backs on me and those who didn't, I am who I am because of you. To Ed Kelly, my former law partner. You are the most compassionate, honorable and loyal friend I have ever been blest to know. And to all of the students and law professors at Roger Williams University, in Bristol Rhode Island, from 1996 to 1999, thank you for a first-class education on and off campus.

ABOUT THE AUTHOR

Michelle Berthiaume

Michelle Berthiaume was born and educated in the Northeastern United States. She enlisted into the armed forces shortly after high school and served in the United States Air Force Security Services, flying special operations missions as crewmember under the direction of the secretive National Security Agency, from 1976 through 1980. She received a certificate in Russian Studies from the Defense Language Institute Foreign Language Center at the Presidio in Monterey California. She earned the Flight medal for flying sensitive special operations missions during the cold war.

Ms Berthiaume later attended several specialized training schools all over the world, including altitude indoctrination and ejection seat qualification courses at McDill Air Force Base in Tampa, Florida, water survival training in Miami, Florida, Wilderness Survival in Spokane, Washington, and an NBC course at Ft. Devens, Massachusetts. She was appointed and completed Officer Candidate School at the Vermont Military Academy, where she was commissioned a Second Lieutenant in the U.S. Army. She attended and completed two separate officer basic courses. One in Fort Huachuca Arizona for tactical intelligence officers, the other at Fort Knox, Kentucky as an armor officer. She served in the Vermont Guard in varying capacities, including scout platoon leader, the Intelligence Officer (S2), NBC training officer at the Battalion level, and as an executive officer and acting company commander of an Armor unit.

While stationed at Offutt AFB, in Omaha, Nebraska, she attended and graduated cum laude from the University of Nebraska. Besides her bachelors, Ms Berthiaume has received an associate's degree in data Processing/computer science from Champlain College, in Burlington, Vermont. She received her Juris Doctor from Roger Williams University in 1999; where she was on Law Review, and the editor-in-chief of their award-winning law school magazine—the Docket.

She has successfully managed a family business that grossed over a million dollars annually and worked as a statistician, an assistant chef, a real estate broker, a division one high school soccer coach, a collections agent, and executive assistant to a partner in a CPA firm in Connecticut. She traveled and worked as a freelance journalist throughout the Northeast before passing the bar and working as an assistant public defender in Fort Myers, Florida, where she distinguished herself by performing more jury trials than any other attorney in the five counties of the Twentieth Judicial District in her first year. She also wrote and won several appeals that influenced Florida law, during that time, and afterwards in private practice.

Her career spanned more than ten years (1999 to 2011) and in that time she was on television, or in the print media continuously with high profile and interesting cases. She now lives in Texas, retired and spends her time traveling and visiting her three daughters and four grandchildren, teaching and writing her memoirs, and self-discovery books to help others find their greatest potential.

Works in Progress:
1) Fyrecurl: a memoir
2) The Light at the End of the World: (biography of an Irish Dreamer)

Made in the USA
Coppell, TX
23 June 2026

82352790R00056